Authors' acknowledgments

Many people contributed to the development of *Four Corners*. The authors and publisher would like to particularly thank the following **reviewers**:

Nele Noe, **Academy for Educational Development, Qatar Independent Secondary School for Girls**, Doha, Qatar; Yuan-hsun Chuang, **Soo Chow University**, Taipei, Taiwan; Celso Frade and Sonia Maria Baccari de Godoy, **Associaçao Alumni**, São Paulo, Brazil; Pablo Stucchi, **Antonio Raimondi School** and **Instituto San Ignacio de Loyola**, Lima, Peru; Kari Miller, **Binational Center**, Quito, Ecuador; Alex K. Oliveira, **Boston University**, Boston, MA, USA; Elisabeth Blom, **Casa Thomas Jefferson**, Brasilia, Brazil; Henry Grant, **CCBEU – Campinas**, Campinas, Brazil; Maria do Rosário, **CCBEU – Franca**, Franca, Brazil; Ane Cibele Palma, **CCBEU Inter Americano**, Curitiba, Brazil; Elen Flavia Penques da Costa, **Centro de Cultura Idiomas – Taubate**, Taubate, Brazil; Inara Lúcia Castillo Couto, **CEL LEP – São Paulo**, São Paulo, Brazil; Geysa de Azevedo Moreira, **Centro Cultural Brasil Estados Unidos (CCBEU Belém)**, Belém, Brazil; Sonia Patricia Cardoso, **Centro de Idiomas Universidad Manuela Beltrán**, Barrio Cedritos, Colombia; Geraldine Itiago Losada, **Centro Universitario Grupo Sol (Musali)**, Mexico City, Mexico; Nick Hilmers, **DePaul University**, Chicago, IL, USA; Monica L. Montemayor Menchaca, **EDIMSA**, Metepec, Mexico; Angela Whitby, **Edu-Idiomas Language School**, Cholula, Puebla, Mexico; Mary Segovia, **El Monte Rosemead Adult School**, Rosemead, CA, USA; Dr. Deborah Aldred, **ELS Language Centers, Middle East Region**, Abu Dhabi, United Arab Emirates; Leslie Lott, **Embassy CES**, Ft. Lauderdale, FL, USA; M. Martha Lengeling, **Escuela de Idiomas**, Guanajuato, Mexico; Pablo Frias, **Escuela de Idiomas UNAPEC**, Santo Domingo, Dominican Republic; Tracy Vanderhoek, **ESL Language Center**, Toronto, Canada; Kris Vicca and Michael McCollister, **Feng Chia University**, Taichung, Taiwan; Flávia Patricia do Nascimento Martins, **First Idiomas**, Sorocaba, Brazil; Andrea Taylor, **Florida State University in Panama**, Panamá, Panama; Carlos Lizárraga González, **Grupo Educativo Angloamericano**, Mexico City, Mexico; Dr. Martin Endley, **Hanyang University**, Seoul, Korea; Mauro Luiz Pinheiro, **IBEU Ceará**, Ceará, Brazil; Ana Lúcia da Costa Maia de Almeida, **IBEU Copacabana**, Copacabana, Brazil; Ana Lucia Almeida, Elisa Borges, **IBEU Rio**, Rio de Janeiro, Brazil; Maristela Silva, **ICBEU Manaus**, Manaus, Brazil; Magaly Mendes Lemos, **ICBEU São José dos Campos**, São José dos Campos, Brazil; Augusto Pelligrini Filho, **ICBEU São Luis**, São Luis, Brazil; Leonardo Mercado, **ICPNA**, Lima, Peru; Lucia Rangel Lugo, **Instituto Tecnológico de San Luis Potosí**, San Luis Potosí, Mexico; Maria Guadalupe Hernández Lozada, **Instituto Tecnológico de Tlalnepantla**, Tlalnepantla de Baz, Mexico; Greg Jankunis, **International Education Service**, Tokyo, Japan; Karen Stewart, **International House Veracruz**, Veracruz, Mexico; George Truscott, **Kinki University**, Osaka, Japan; Bo-Kyung Lee, **Hankuk University of Foreign Studies**, Seoul, Korea; Andy Burki, **Korea University, International Foreign Language School**, Seoul, Korea; Jinseo Noh, **Kwangwoon University**, Seoul, Korea; Nadezhda Nazarenko, **Lone Star College**, Houston, TX, USA; Carolyn Ho, **Lone Star College-Cy-Fair**, Cypress, TX, USA; Alice Ya-fen Chou, **National Taiwan University of Science and Technology**, Taipei, Taiwan; Gregory Hadley, **Niigata University of International and Information Studies, Department of Information Culture**, Niigata-shi, Japan; Raymond Dreyer, **Northern Essex Community College**, Lawrence, MA, USA; Mary Keter Terzian Megale, **One Way Línguas-Suzano**, São Paulo, Brazil; Jason Moser, **Osaka Shoin Joshi University**, Kashiba-shi, Japan; Bonnie Cheeseman, **Pasadena Community College** and **UCLA American Language Center**, Los Angeles, CA, USA; Simon Banha, **Phil Young's English School**, Curitiba, Brazil; Oh Jun Il, **Pukyong National University**, Busan, Korea; Carmen Gehrke, **Quatrum English Schools**, Porto Alegre, Brazil; Atsuko K. Yamazaki, **Shibaura Institute of Technology**, Saitama, Japan; Wen hsiang Su, **Shi Chien University, Kaohsiung Campus**, Kaohsiung, Taiwan; Richmond Stroupe, **Soka University, World Language Center**, Hachioji, Tokyo, Japan; Lynne Kim, **Sun Moon University (Institute for Language Education)**, Cheon An City, Chung Nam, Korea; Hiroko Nishikage, **Taisho University**, Tokyo, Japan; Diaña Peña Munoz and Zaira Kuri, **The Anglo**, Mexico City, Mexico; Alistair Campbell, **Tokyo University of Technology**, Tokyo, Japan; Song-won Kim, **TTI (Teacher's Training Institute)**, Seoul, Korea; Nancy Alarcón, **UNAM FES Zaragoza Language Center**, Mexico City, Mexico; Laura Emilia Fierro López, **Universidad Autónoma de Baja California**, Mexicali, Mexico; María del Rocío Domíngeuz Gaona, **Universidad Autónoma de Baja California**, Tijuana, Mexico; Saul Santos Garcia, **Universidad Autónoma de Nayarit**, Nayarit, Mexico; Christian Meléndez, **Universidad Católica de El Salvador**, San Salvador, El Salvador; Irasema Mora Pablo, **Universidad de Guanajuato**, Guanajuato, Mexico; Alberto Peto, **Universidad de Oxaca**, Tehuantepec, Mexico; Carolina Rodriguez Beltan, **Universidad Manuela Beltrán, Centro Colombo Americano**, and **Universidad Jorge Tadeo Lozano**, Bogotá, Colombia; Nidia Milena Molina Rodriguez, **Universidad Manuela Beltrán** and **Universidad Militar Nueva Granada**, Bogotá, Colombia; Yolima Perez Arias, **Universidad Nacional de Colombia**, Bogota, Colombia; Héctor Vázquez García, **Universidad Nacional Autónoma de Mexico**, Mexico City, Mexico; Pilar Barrera, **Universidad Técnica de Ambato**, Ambato, Ecuador; Deborah Hulston, **University of Regina**, Regina, Canada; Rebecca J. Shelton, **Valparaiso University, Interlink Language Center**, Valparaiso, IN, USA; Tae Lee, **Yonsei University**, Seodaemun-gu, Seoul, Korea; Claudia Thereza Nascimento Mendes, **York Language Institute**, Rio de Janeiro, Brazil; Jamila Jenny Hakam, **ELT Consultant**, Muscat, Oman; Stephanie Smith, **ELT Consultant**, Austin, TX, USA.

The authors would also like to thank the Four Corners editorial, production, and new media teams, as well as the Cambridge University Press staff and advisors around the world for their contributions and tireless commitment to quality.

Scope and sequence

LEVEL 1B	Learning outcomes	Grammar	Vocabulary
Unit 7 Pages 65–74			
Food A *Breakfast, lunch, and dinner* B *I like Chinese food!* C *Meals* D *Favorite food*	**Students can . . .** ☑ say what meals they eat ☑ say what they like and dislike ☑ talk about their eating habits ☑ talk about their favorite food	Count and noncount nouns *Some* and *any* *How often* Time expressions	Food More food
Unit 8 Pages 75–84			
In the neighborhood A *Around town* B *How do I get to . . . ?* C *Fun in the city* D *A great place to visit*	**Students can . . .** ☑ give the locations of neighborhood places ☑ ask for and give directions ☑ talk about interesting places in their towns ☑ give a presentation on a city attraction	Prepositions of location *There is, there are*	Places in the neighborhood Places to visit
Unit 9 Pages 85–94			
What are you doing? A *I'm looking for you.* B *I can't talk right now.* C *These days* D *What's new?*	**Students can . . .** ☑ describe what people are doing right now ☑ ask if someone can talk now ☑ explain why they can't talk on the telephone ☑ describe what people are doing these days ☑ discuss what people are doing	Present continuous statements Present continuous questions	Actions and prepositions Activities
Unit 10 Pages 95–104			
Past experiences A *Last weekend* B *You're kidding!* C *Did you make dinner last night?* D *I saw a great movie.*	**Students can . . .** ☑ say what they did last weekend ☑ show that they're listening ☑ express surprise ☑ talk about routine events in the past ☑ talk about past activities	Simple past regular verbs Simple past irregular verbs *Yes / no* questions	Weekend activities Things to do
Unit 11 Pages 105–114			
Getting away A *Where were you?* B *That's great!* C *My vacation* D *Travel experiences*	**Students can . . .** ☑ describe where they were in the past ☑ react to news ☑ talk about their last vacation ☑ describe a vacation	Past of *be* Simple past *Wh-* questions	Adjectives Vacation activities
Unit 12 Pages 115–124			
Time to celebrate A *I'm going to get married.* B *Sure. I'd love to.* C *Planning a party* D *Birthdays*	**Students can . . .** ☑ talk about their plans for specific dates ☑ accept or decline an invitation ☑ discuss and agree on plans ☑ describe birthday traditions in their cultures	*Be going to* *Yes / no* questions *Wh-* questions with *be going to* Object pronouns	Months and dates Party checklist

Classroom language

Pair work

Group work

Class activity

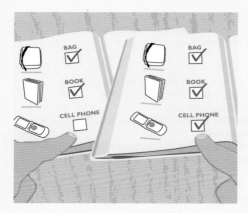

Compare answers.

Cover the picture.

Go to page 12.

What's your name?

My name is Marisa.

Ask and answer questions.

Interview your partner.

Role-play the situation.

Food

LESSON **A**	LESSON **B**	LESSON **C**	LESSON **D**
• Food • Count and noncount nouns; *some* and *any*	• Expressing likes • Expressing dislikes	• More food • *How often*; time expressions	• Reading: An article • Writing: A typical meal

Warm-up

A Match the words and the pictures.

1. Italian food <u>c</u>   2. Mexican food ____   3. Chinese food ____   4. Japanese food ____

B Name ten food words you know.

1 Vocabulary Food

A 🔊 Match the words and the pictures. Then listen and check your answers.

a. apples	e. carrots	i. eggs	m. pasta
b. bananas	f. cereal	j. fish	n. potatoes
c. beans	✓g. cheese	k. milk	o. rice
d. beef	h. chicken	l. noodles	p. tomatoes

Dairy

1. g 2. ☐

Vegetables

3. ☐ 4. ☐ 5. ☐

Fruit

6. ☐ 7. ☐

Grains

8. ☐ 9. ☐ 10. ☐ 11. ☐

Meat and Protein

12. ☐ 13. ☐ 14. ☐ 15. ☐ 16. ☐

B Pair work Do you ever eat the food in Part A? Tell your partner.

"I often eat apples. I sometimes eat eggs. I never eat noodles."

2 Language in context Favorite meals

A 🔊 Listen to three people talk about their favorite meals. Underline the food words.

I love breakfast. I usually eat some cereal, but I don't have any milk with it. I also eat an apple.

My favorite meal is lunch. I don't have a lot of time, so I often just get some noodles.

My favorite meal of the day is dinner. A typical dinner for me is rice and beans with some beef.

B What about you? What's your favorite meal of the day? What do you eat?

3 Grammar 🔊 Count and noncount nouns; *some* and *any*

Count nouns		Noncount nouns	

Count nouns

an apple   a tomato

apples   tomatoes

Do you have **any** apples?
  Yes, I have **some** (apples).
  No, I don't have **any** (apples).

Noncount nouns

milk   cereal

Do you have **any** milk?
  Yes, I have **some** (milk).
  No, I don't have **any** (milk).

A Complete the chart with the food words from Exercise 1. Then compare with a partner.

Count nouns		Noncount nouns	
apples	_____	milk	_____
tomatoes	_____	cereal	_____
_____	_____	_____	_____
_____	_____	_____	_____

B Circle the correct words. Then practice with a partner.

A: What do you want for lunch, Amy?
B: Let's just make (some) / **any** pasta.
A: Good idea. We have **some** / **any** pasta.
B: Let's see. We have **some** / **any** carrots. We don't
  have **some** / **any** tomatoes.
A: OK, I can get **some** / **any** at the store. What else?
B: Do we have **some** / **any** cheese?
A: No, we don't have **some** / **any**. I can get **some** / **any**.

C Pair work Practice the conversation again. Use other
food words from Exercise 1.

4 Speaking What do you eat?

A Write your answers to the questions in the chart.

What do you often eat for . . . ?	Me	Name: _____	Name: _____
breakfast			
lunch			
dinner			

B Group work Interview two classmates. Complete the chart with their answers.

5 Keep talking!

Go to page 139 for more practice.

I can say what meals I eat. ☑

B I like Chinese food!

1 Interactions — Likes and dislikes

A Look at the pictures. Where are Maria and Tom?

B 🔊 Listen and practice.

Maria: Do you like pasta?
Tom: No, I don't like Italian food.

Maria: How about Chinese food?
Tom: Good idea. I like Chinese food!

C 🔊 Listen to the expressions. Then practice the conversation again with the new expressions.

Expressing dislikes

 I don't like . . .

 I don't like . . . at all.

 I hate . . . !

Expressing likes

 I like . . .

 I really like . . .

 I love . . . !

D Pair work Look at Maria's and Tom's likes and dislikes. Are they the same as yours? Tell your partner.

	😍	😃	🙂	🙁	😟	😣
Maria	fish	Mexican food	Japanese food	milk	beans	beef
Tom	cheese	carrots	Chinese food	Italian food	French food	eggs

"Maria loves fish, but I don't like fish at all."

2 Pronunciation Word stress

A 🔊 Listen and repeat. Notice the stress in the words.

●	●·	·●·
cheese	**a**pple	ba**na**na
beans	**chi**cken	po**ta**to
beef	**noo**dles	to**ma**to
_____	_____	_____
_____	_____	_____

B 🔊 Listen. Complete the chart with the correct words.

dairy   fruit   Italian   meat   pasta

3 Listening I love it!

A 🔊 Listen to four conversations about food. Check (✓) the words you hear.

1. ☐ beans   2. ☐ cheese   3. ☐ noodles   4. ☐ bananas
   ✓ beef   ☐ chicken   ☐ potatoes   ☐ carrots
   ✓ pasta   ☐ eggs   ☐ tomatoes   ☐ cereal

B 🔊 Listen again. Do the two speakers like the same things?
Circle the correct answers.

1. yes / (no)   2. yes / no   3. yes / no   4. yes / no

4 Speaking What do you like?

A Make a list of food you like and food you don't like.

Food I like	Food I don't like
🙂	🙁
😀	😖
😍	😣

B **Pair work** Tell your partner about the food you like and don't like.
Ask and answer questions for more information.

A: _I really like fish._
B: _Do you cook fish at home?_
A: _No, I don't. I eat fish in restaurants._

I can say what I like and dislike. ☑

C Meals

1 Vocabulary More food

A 🔊 Label the pictures with the correct words. Then listen and check your answers.

dumplings	✓hot dogs	pizza	soup	sushi
hamburgers	pancakes	salad	spaghetti	tacos

1. _hot dogs_   2. _____   3. _____   4. _____   5. _____

6. _____   7. _____   8. _____   9. _____   10. _____

B Pair work Which food in Part A do you like? Which food don't you like? Compare your answers.

A: *I really like dumplings. Do you?*
B: *Yes, I like dumplings, too. Do you like . . . ?*

2 Conversation I eat pizza every day.

🔊 Listen and practice.

Megan: What is that?
David: Pizza. My father is a pizza chef.
Megan: Really? So how often do you eat pizza?
David: I eat pizza every day. It's my favorite food!
Megan: I don't eat pizza very often, but it looks interesting. What's on it?
David: Cheese, tomatoes, black beans, and fish.
Megan: Black beans and fish on pizza. Yuck!
David: Have some. It's really good.
Megan: No, thanks. I'm not very hungry.

3 Grammar 🔊 *How often;* time expressions

How often do you eat pizza?

| I eat pizza | every day.
once a week.
twice a month.
three times a month.
once in a while. | I do**n't** eat pizza **very often**.
I **never** eat pizza. |

A Look at Matt's menu. Answer the questions. Then practice with a partner.

Matt's Menu

	Monday	Tuesday	Wednesday	Thursday	Friday	Saturday	Sunday
Breakfast	cereal	eggs	cereal	eggs	cereal	pancakes	pancakes
Lunch	soup	pizza	soup	sushi	soup	tacos	sushi
Dinner	dumplings	chicken	beef	chicken	pizza	spaghetti	hamburgers

1. How often does Matt eat hamburgers for dinner?   *He eats hamburgers once a week.*
2. How often does Matt eat soup for lunch?   _____
3. How often does Matt eat pancakes?   _____
4. How often does Matt eat hot dogs?   _____
5. How often does Matt eat sushi for lunch?   _____
6. How often does Matt eat dumplings for dinner?   _____

B **Pair work** Make six sentences about your eating habits with different time expressions. Tell your partner.

"I eat spaghetti once a month."

4 Speaking Eating habits

A Add three food words to the chart. Then answer the questions.

How often do you eat . . . ?	Me	Name: _____
hot dogs		
salad		
tacos		

B **Pair work** Interview your partner. Complete the chart with his or her answers.

C **Pair work** Compare your information with another partner.

"Kazu eats hot dogs once a week, but I eat them once in a while."

5 Keep talking!

Go to page **140** for more practice.

I **can** talk about my eating habits. ☑

D Favorite food

1 Reading 🔊

A Look at the pictures in the magazine article. Can you name the food?

B Read the article. What's the best title? Check (✓) the correct answer.

☐ Meal Times   ☐ My Favorite Food   ☐ Dinner Around the World

Letters from our readers

I love nachos. I make them once a week. I just buy some tortilla chips and put cheese, beef, tomatoes, and onions on top. Then I cook it in the microwave.

HEATHER
United States

I like dumplings a lot. You can buy good dumplings in restaurants, but I usually eat my mother's dumplings. They're delicious! I eat them for lunch four or five times a month.

JAE-SUN
South Korea

My wife and I go to our favorite ice-cream shop three times a month. They have many flavors, but we always get chocolate ice cream. It's our favorite.

CARLOS
Argentina

I really like pancakes, but we don't eat them for breakfast. We eat them after dinner. We usually eat them two or three times a month. I like to eat them with jam.

OLGA
Sweden

C Read the article again. Complete the chart with the correct information.

	Favorite food	How often they have it
Heather	*nachos*	*once a week*
Jae-sun		
Carlos		
Olga		

D Pair work Imagine you can have one food in Part A right now. Which food do you want? Why? Tell your partner.

"I want dumplings. I love Korean food. Vegetable dumplings are my favorite."

2 Listening A meal in Sweden

A 🔊 Listen to Olga describe a typical meal in Sweden.
Which meal does she talk about? Check (✓) the correct answer.

☐ breakfast   ☐ lunch   ☐ dinner

B 🔊 Listen again. Circle the words you hear.

beans	(bread)	cheese	fish	milk	pancakes
beef	cereal	eggs	fruit	noodles	potatoes

3 Writing A typical meal

A Think of a typical meal in your country. Answer the questions.

• What do people drink? _____

• What do people eat? _____

• Do *you* usually eat it? _____

• Why or why not? _____

B Write about a typical meal in your country.
Use the model and your answers in Part A to help you.

C **Class activity** Post your writing around the room.
Read your classmates' writing. Who describes similar meals?

> *A Japanese Breakfast*
> *People in Japan usually drink green tea for breakfast. They eat fish, rice, soup, salad, and pickles. It's a healthy and delicious breakfast, but I don't eat this. I usually drink orange juice and eat cereal and fruit for breakfast.*

4 Speaking What's your favorite meal?

A **Pair work** Add two questions about food to the chart. Then interview your partner. Take notes.

Questions	Name: _____
What's your favorite meal?	
What's your favorite kind of food?	
How often do you have it?	
Who makes it?	
Can you cook it?	
What do you drink with it?	

A: *What's your favorite kind of food?*
B: *I love Mexican food.*

B **Group work** Tell your group about your partner's favorite meal.
Do you like that meal, too? Does your group like it?

I can talk about my favorite food. ✓

73

Wrap-up

1 Quick pair review

Lesson A Brainstorm! Make a list of count and noncount food words. How many do you know? You have one minute.

Lesson B Do you remember? Look at the pictures. Complete the sentences with the correct words. You have one minute.

☹ I _don't like_ fish _at all_ .　　☺ I _____ French food.

☹ I _____ _____ beef.　　☺ I _____ _____ breakfast.

☹ I _____ milk!　　☺ I _____ carrots!

Lesson C Find out! What is one thing both you and your partner eat every week? eat once in a while? never eat? You have two minutes.

A: *I eat rice every week. Do you?*
B: *Yes, I do.*

Lesson D Guess! Describe your favorite food, but don't say its name! Can your partner guess what it is? Take turns. You have two minutes.

A: *I love this food. It's Italian, and I eat it once in a while. I eat it at home.*
B: *Is it pasta?*
A: *Yes.*

2 In the real world

Go online and find information in English about your favorite movie star's or musician's eating habits. Then write about them.

- What is his or her favorite food?
- How often does he or she usually eat it?

> *Jack Black's Favorite Food*
> *The American actor Jack Black doesn't have one favorite food. He has two of them! He loves pizza and cheeseburgers.*

In the neighborhood

Warm-up

A Look at the picture. Make six sentences about it.

B Where can you do these things?

| buy glasses | buy some fruit | check email | eat lunch | get a book | see a movie |

1 Vocabulary Places in the neighborhood

A 🔊 Match the words and the places. Then listen and check your answers.

a. bank	c. bus stop	e. gas station	✓g. library	i. subway station
b. bookstore	d. coffee shop	f. hotel	h. newsstand	j. supermarket

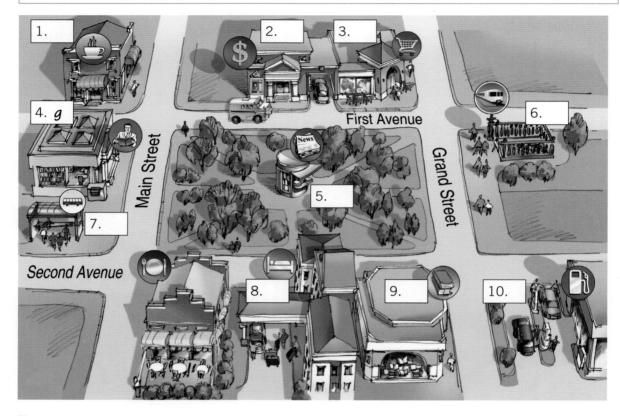

1.
2.
3.
4. *g*
5.
6.
7.
8.
9.
10.

First Avenue
Main Street
Grand Street
Second Avenue
News

B **Pair work** Which places are in your school's neighborhood?

"We have a coffee shop, some restaurants, and a . . ."

2 Language in context Ads

A 🔊 Read three advertisements for places in a neighborhood. What places do they describe?

Mama's Place

Come to Mama's Place for real Italian food.

On Second Avenue
10% off
between 5:30 and 6:30 p.m.

ABC Supermarket
WE'RE ALWAYS OPEN!

Find everything you need at ABC Supermarket!

New location next to Town Bank

JOE'S COFFEE SHOP

Best coffee in town!
Find us on the corner of Main St. and First Ave.

B What can you do at each place in Part A?

3 Grammar 🔊 | Prepositions of location

     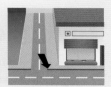

| in | on | next to | across from | between | on the corner of |

The newsstand is **in** the park.
The gas station is **on** Second Avenue.
The supermarket is **next to** the bank.
The bus stop is **across from** the park.

The hotel is **between** the restaurant and the bookstore.
The coffee shop is **on the corner of** Main Street and First Avenue.

Look at the map in Exercise 1. Complete the sentences with the correct prepositions.

1. The newsstand is _____*in*_____ the park.
2. The subway station is _____ the park.
3. The bookstore is _____ the hotel.
4. Mama's Place is _____ Second Avenue.
5. The gas station is _____ Second Avenue and Grand Street.
6. The library is _____ the coffee shop and the bus stop.

4 Pronunciation Word stress

🔊 Listen and repeat. Notice the stress on the first or last syllable.

●●		●●
bookstore	**news**stand	a**cross**
coffee	**sta**tion	be**tween**
corner	**sub**way	ho**tel**

5 Speaking Where's the drugstore?

A Pair work Add these four places to the map in Exercise 1. Then ask and answer questions about their locations.

| drugstore | post office | Internet café | department store |

A: *Where's the drugstore on your map?*
B: *It's next to the bank. Where is it on your map?*

B Pair work Where are the places in your town? Tell your partner.

6 Keep talking!

Student A go to page 141 and Student B go to page 142 for more practice.

I can **give the locations of neighborhood places.** ✓

1 Giving directions

A 🔊 Listen and repeat.

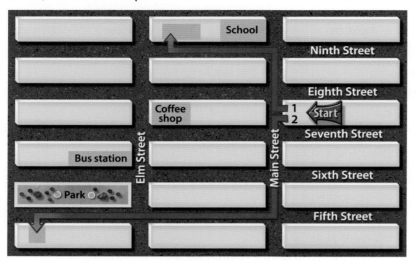

1
Go up Main Street.
Turn left on Ninth Street.
Go one block.
It's **on the right**, next to a school.

2
Walk down Main Street.
Take a right on Fifth Street.
Walk two blocks.
It's **on the left**, across from the park.

B **Pair work** Give directions from *Start* to the coffee shop and the bus station.

2 Interactions   Directions

A 🔊 Listen and practice.

Alex: Excuse me. How do I get to the park?
Laura: Go down Seventh Street and take a left on Elm Street. Walk one block to Sixth Street. It's on the right, across from the bus station.
Alex: Turn left on Elm Street?
Laura: Yes.
Alex: Great! Thank you very much.

B 🔊 Listen to the expressions. Then practice the conversation again with the new expression.

Asking for directions

How do I get to . . . ?
How can I get to . . . ?

3 Listening Follow the route

A 🔊 Listen to Carl and Alice use their GPS to get from Pioneer Square to the library in Seattle. Follow their route. Then mark an ✗ at the library.

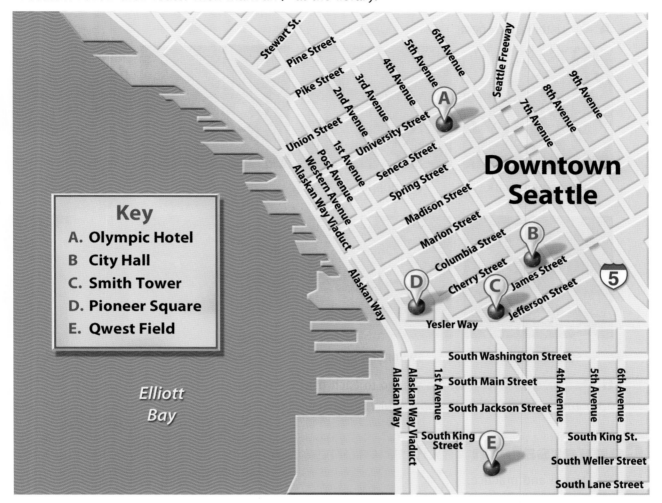

Key
A. Olympic Hotel
B City Hall
C. Smith Tower
D. Pioneer Square
E. Qwest Field

B 🔊 Listen to Carl and Alice go from the library to Pike Place Market. Follow their route. Then mark a ✓ at the market.

C Pair work Give directions from Pioneer Square to other places on the map. Your partner follows them. Take turns.

4 Speaking How do I get to . . . ?

A Pair work Draw a simple map of the neighborhood around your school. Label different places and street names.

B Pair work Role-play the situation. Then change roles.

Student A: You are a tourist in town. Ask for directions to places in the neighborhood.
Student B: You meet a tourist in your town. Give him or her directions to places in your neighborhood. Start at your school.

A: *How do I get to the train station?*
B: *Walk down Main Street . . .*

I can ask for and give directions. ✓

C Fun in the city

1 Vocabulary Places to visit

A 🔊 Listen and repeat.

amusement park

aquarium

movie theater

museum

science center

swimming pool

water park

zoo

B **Pair work** How often do you go to each place? Tell your partner.

"Our town has a swimming pool, but I hardly ever go there."

2 Conversation Tourist information

🔊 Listen and practice.

Larry: Hello. Can I help you?

Maggie: Yes. Is there a museum near here?

Larry: Let's see. . . . Yes. There's a museum across from the park.

Maggie: And is there an aquarium in this city?

Larry: Yes, there is. It's near the museum. It's a very nice aquarium.

Maggie: Great. I have one more question. Are there any amusement parks?

Larry: There aren't any amusement parks, but there's a nice water park.

3 Grammar ◄)) **There is, there are**

There's a museum.	**There are** two swimming pools.
There isn't an amusement park.	**There aren't** any good zoos in this city.
Is there an aquarium in this city?	**Are there** any swimming pools near here?
Yes, **there is.** No, **there isn't.**	Yes, **there are.** No, **there aren't.**

Contraction There's = There is

A Complete the questions about the city with *Is there a / an . . . ?* or
Are there any . . . ? Then compare with a partner.

1. *Is there a* _____ zoo?
2. _____ water parks?
3. _____ aquarium?
4. _____ museums?
5. _____ amusement park?
6. _____ movie theaters?

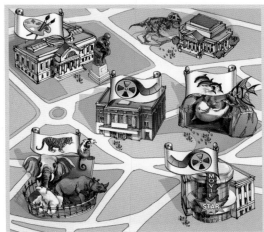

B Pair work Ask and answer the questions in Part A.
Use the map on the right.

   A: *Is there a zoo?*
   B: *Yes, there is. There's one zoo.*

4 Speaking Is there . . . ? Are there . . . ?

A Pair work Add two items to the chart. Then interview your partner. Check (✓)
the places that are in his or her neighborhood, and ask for more information.

	Places	Locations	Extra information
☐	movie theaters		
☐	museums		
☐	science center		
☐	swimming pool		
☐			
☐			

   A: *Are there any movie theaters in your neighborhood?*
   B: *Yes, there's one. It's on University Avenue.*
   A: *How often do you go there?*

B Class activity Tell the class about two interesting places in your
partner's neighborhood.

5 Keep talking!

Go to page 143 for more practice.

I can *talk about interesting places in my town.* ☑

D A great place to visit

1 Reading 🔊

A Is there an aquarium in your town or city? If yes, do you like it? If no, do you want one?

B Read the poster. Where is the Monterey Bay Aquarium?

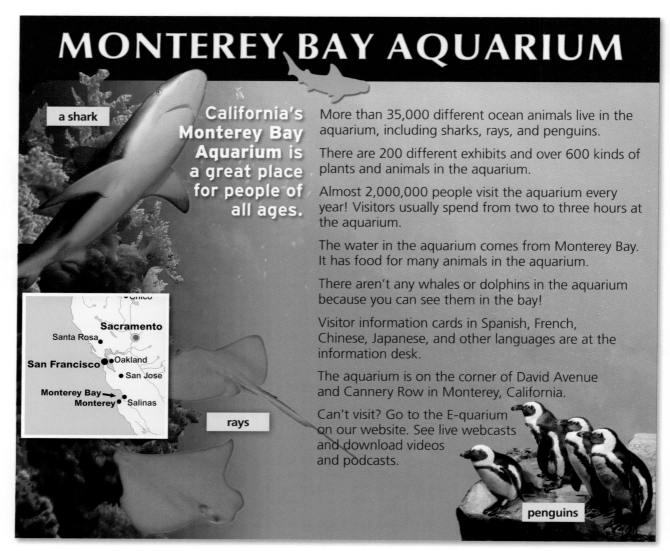

MONTEREY BAY AQUARIUM

a shark

California's Monterey Bay Aquarium is a great place for people of all ages.

More than 35,000 different ocean animals live in the aquarium, including sharks, rays, and penguins.

There are 200 different exhibits and over 600 kinds of plants and animals in the aquarium.

Almost 2,000,000 people visit the aquarium every year! Visitors usually spend from two to three hours at the aquarium.

The water in the aquarium comes from Monterey Bay. It has food for many animals in the aquarium.

There aren't any whales or dolphins in the aquarium because you can see them in the bay!

Visitor information cards in Spanish, French, Chinese, Japanese, and other languages are at the information desk.

The aquarium is on the corner of David Avenue and Cannery Row in Monterey, California.

Can't visit? Go to the E-quarium on our website. See live webcasts and download videos and podcasts.

Sacramento, Santa Rosa, San Francisco, Oakland, San Jose, Monterey Bay, Monterey, Salinas

rays

penguins

C Read the poster again. Answer the questions.

1. What animals live in the aquarium? _Sharks, rays, and penguins live in the aquarium._
2. Where does the aquarium's water come from? _____
3. Are there any whales or dolphins in the aquarium? _____
4. Where are the visitor information cards? _____
5. What is on their website? _____

D Pair work What is your favorite place to visit in your town or city? Why? Tell your partner.

"I like the modern art museum because it has cool paintings. I go to the museum once a month."

2 Listening City information

A 🔊 Listen to three tourists ask for information about two places in the city.
Write the places in the chart.

	Place 1	Place 2
1.	(movie theater)	
2.		
3.		

B 🔊 Listen again. Which places are in the city? Circle the correct answers.

3 Writing and speaking Group poster presentation

A **Group work** Choose an interesting place in your city. What do you know about it?
Make a list.

B **Group work** Create and design a poster about the place. Use your list from Part A.

COME TO THE IMAGINE SCIENCE CENTER!
Great for kids, teens, and adults.

- *We're open every day from 9:00 to 6:00.*
- *There's a free audio tour in ten languages.*
- *There's an excellent café in the museum.*
- *Try our science experiments.*
- *Learn about plant life.*
- *There are over 10,000 books in the bookstore.*

C **Class activity** Present your posters. Ask and answer questions for
more information.

A: *The Imagine Science Center is a great place to visit.*
B: *It's open every day from 9:00 to 6:00.*
C: *There's a free audio tour. You can listen to the tour in ten languages.*
D: *Where is the Imagine Science Center?*
C: *It's at 367 First Avenue, near the park.*

I can give a presentation on a city attraction. ☑

Wrap-up

1 Quick pair review

Lesson A **Brainstorm!** Make a list of places in a neighborhood. How many do you know? You have one minute.

Lesson B **Do you remember?** Circle the correct answers. You have two minutes.

A: Excuse me. **Where** / **How** do I get to the library from here?
B: Walk up Third Avenue and **turn** / **take** left on Elm Street.
A: Is the library on Elm Street?
B: No, it's not. **Go** / **Turn** two blocks on Elm Street. Then **take** / **walk** a right on Main Street. The library is **on** / **in** the right.
A: Thanks!

Lesson C **Find out!** What are two kinds of places both you and your partner like to visit in your city or other cities? What are two kinds of places you don't like to visit? You have two minutes.

A: *I like museums. Do you?*
B: *Not really. How about water parks? I love those!*
A: *I do, too!*

Lesson D **Guess!** Describe a place to visit in your area, but don't say its name! Can your partner guess the name? Take turns. You have two minutes.

A: *I go there with my friends on weekends.*
B: *Is it Mall Marina?*
A: *No. There are rides and games there.*
B: *Is it the amusement park, Fantasy Land?*
A: *Yes!*

2 In the real world

What zoos do you know? Go online and find information in English about a zoo. Then write about it.

- What is the name of the zoo? Where is it?
- What animals and exhibits are there?
- Can you watch videos or take a tour on the website?

> *The San Diego Zoo*
> *The San Diego Zoo is a famous zoo in California. You can see pandas there. You can also . . .*

84

What are you doing?

Warm-up

A Look at the picture. Make eight sentences about it.

B Do you ever do these things on a subway, train, or bus?

A I'm looking for you.

1 Vocabulary Actions and prepositions

A 🔊 Listen and repeat.

start   hold   look for   wave

sit   stand   run   end

B 🔊 Listen and repeat.

behind   in   in front of   on   under

C Pair work Tell your partner to sit and stand in different places in the classroom. Use the prepositions. Take turns.

"Stand in front of the door."

2 Language in context Meeting a friend

A 🔊 Listen to Amy and Claudio meet at a soccer game. Where is Amy? Where is Claudio?

Amy: Hi, Claudio. It's Amy. I'm standing under the scoreboard. Where are you?

Claudio: I'm sitting in front of the big clock. Do you see me?

Amy: No, I don't.

Claudio: Well, I'm wearing a red shirt.

Amy: But, Claudio, everyone is wearing a red shirt!

B What about you? Where do you usually meet your friends at big games or other events?

3 Grammar ◄)) Present continuous statements

I**'m standing** under the scoreboard.	I**'m not sitting**.	*Spelling*
You**'re running**.	You**'re not walking**.	run → run**ning**
He**'s sitting** in front of the big clock.	He**'s not standing**.	sit → sit**ting**
It**'s starting**.	It**'s not ending**.	wave → wav**ing**
We**'re holding** scarves.	We**'re not waving**.	
They**'re playing** soccer.	They**'re not playing** tennis.	

A Complete Claudio's text messages with the present continuous forms of the verbs. Then compare with a partner.

1.
> Where are you, Tim?
> I *'m looking* _____
> (look) for you. The game
> _____
> (start), but my favorite
> player _____
> (not / play) right now. Please
> text me.

2.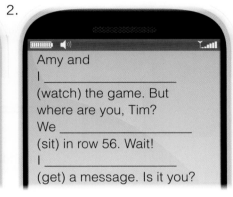
> Amy and
> I _____
> (watch) the game. But
> where are you, Tim?
> We _____
> (sit) in row 56. Wait!
> I _____
> (get) a message. Is it you?

3.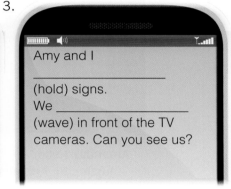
> Amy and I
> _____
> (hold) signs.
> We _____
> (wave) in front of the TV
> cameras. Can you see us?

B **Pair work** Make ten sentences about people in your class with the present continuous. Tell your partner.

"I'm sitting behind Eva. Lily and Mei are wearing sweaters."

4 Listening Someone is . . .

◄)) Listen to the sound effects. What is happening? Circle the correct answers.

1. Someone is (watching a game) / watching a movie.
2. Someone is **getting up** / **going to bed**.
3. Someone is **walking** / **running**.
4. Some people are **playing tennis** / **playing soccer**.
5. The game is **starting** / **ending**.

5 Speaking Guess the action.

Group work Perform an action. Your group guesses it. Take turns.

cook	run	stand
play tennis	sit	watch TV
play the guitar	sleep	wave

A: *You're dancing.*
B: *No, I'm not.*
A: *You're playing soccer.*
B: *Yes, that's right.*

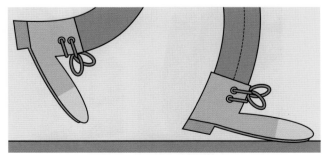

6 Keep talking!

Go to page 144 for more practice.

I can describe what people are doing right now. ☑

B I can't talk right now.

1 Interactions   Can you talk?

A Look at the pictures. What is Amanda doing?

B 🔊 Listen and practice.

Amanda: Hello?
Justin: Hi, Amanda. It's Justin. Is this a good time to talk?

Amanda: Oh, sorry. I can't talk right now. I'm cooking dinner. Can I call you back?
Justin: OK, sure. Talk to you later.
Amanda: Thanks. Bye.

C 🔊 Listen to the expressions. Then practice the conversation again with the new expressions.

Asking if someone can talk now
Is this a good time to talk? Can you talk right now? Do you have a minute?

Explaining that you can't talk now
I can't talk right now. I'm busy right now. This isn't a good time.

D **Pair work** Practice the conversation again with the reasons below.

clean

do my homework

play volleyball

wait for the doctor

2 Listening Do you have a minute?

A 🔊 Listen to four phone conversations. Number the questions you hear from 1 to 4.

_____ Can you talk right now?   _____ Is this a good time to talk?

_____ Is this a good time?   _1_ Do you have a minute?

B 🔊 Listen again. Why can't each person talk right now? Write the reason.

1. Eric _is having dinner_ .   3. Ji-won _____ .

2. Renee _____ .   4. Carmen _____ .

3 Speaking Role play

A Complete the sentences with reasons why you can't talk on the phone.

I'm watching _____ .   I'm eating _____ .

I'm playing _____ .   I'm _____ .

B **Pair work** Role-play the situations. Then change roles.

Student A: Answer the phone. Explain that you can't talk now and say why. Use the reasons from Part A.

Student B: Call Student A. Identify yourself and ask if he or she can talk right now.

I can **ask if someone can talk now.** ✓

I can **explain why I can't talk on the telephone.** ✓

1 Vocabulary Activities

A 🔊 Listen and repeat.

create a website

learn to drive

look for a job

study for an exam

study Italian

take a dance class

take tennis lessons

tutor a student

B Pair work Which activities are fun? Which are not fun? Compare answers with a partner.

2 Conversation Old friends

🔊 Listen and practice.

Jill: Long time no see, Wendy!
Wendy: Oh, hi, Jill.
Jill: What are you doing these days?
Wendy: I'm learning to drive. I'm also tutoring a student. Oh, and I'm taking a dance class.
Jill: You sound really busy.
Wendy: I am. How about you, Jill? Are *you* doing anything special these days?
Jill: Yes, I am. I'm studying Italian.
Wendy: Really? Why are you studying Italian?
Jill: Because . . . Oh, my phone is ringing. Hello? Sorry, Wendy. It's my new friend, Luigi.
Wendy: Oh.
Jill: *Ciao, Luigi! Come stai?*

3 Grammar 🔊 Present continuous questions

What **are** you **doing** these days?
   I**'m learning** to drive.
What class **is** Wendy **taking**?
   She**'s taking** a dance class.
Where **are** they **studying**?
   They**'re studying** online.
	Are you **doing** anything special these days?
	   Yes, I **am**. No, I**'m not**.
	Is she **tutoring** a student?
	   Yes, she **is**. No, she**'s not**.
	Are they **taking** tennis lessons?
	   Yes, they **are**. No, they**'re not**.

A Complete the questions with the present continuous forms of the verbs.
Then compare with a partner.

1. ___*Are*___ you ___*taking*___ (take) music lessons these days?
2. What classes _____ you _____ (take)?
3. _____ you and your friends _____ (buy) CDs these days?
4. What _____ your classmates _____ (learn) in this class?
5. What languages _____ you _____ (study)?
6. _____ you _____ (learn) to drive?

B Pair work Ask and answer the questions in Part A. Answer with your own information.

4 Pronunciation Intonation in questions

🔊 Listen and repeat. Notice the intonation of *yes / no* and *Wh-* questions.

Are you watching a lot of TV?   What TV shows are you watching?

5 Speaking Busy lives

Class activity Add two activities to the chart. Then find classmates who are doing each thing these days. Write their names, and ask questions for more information.

Are you . . . these days?	Name	Extra information
studying another language		
reading a good book		
watching a lot of TV		
taking any fun classes		
downloading a lot of music		

6 Keep talking!

Go to page **145** for more practice.

I can *describe what people are doing these days.* ☑

D What's new?

1 Reading 🔊

A What are you and your classmates doing right now?

B Read the status updates. Which two people are waiting for other people?

Status Updates

SIGN UP | **SIGN IN** | **SEARCH**

What are you doing?

Donna Bristol I'm standing under the JB Cola sign on Main Street. I'm waiting for my friend Hank. But Hank is never late! Hank?
Apr 19 8:33 p.m.

Hank Jones I'm standing in line. Donna, please wait!! I'm in a store on First Avenue. The line isn't moving.
Apr 19 8:50 p.m.

Fernando Sanchez I'm studying English. I'm doing grammar exercises on my DVD-ROM. I'm getting them all correct. Yay!
Apr 19 9:05 p.m.

Zack Parker I'm enjoying Singapore!! I love vacations! How are my friends in Chicago doing?
Apr 19 9:17 p.m.

Hee-jin Park I'm having a great evening. I'm at my favorite restaurant with my two friends Alex and Eddie. We're waiting for dessert.
Apr 19 9:28 p.m.

Jessica King I'm looking for a good French dictionary. I'm taking a French class and need help with my vocabulary.
Apr 19 9:44 p.m.

Arthur Henderson I'm waiting for my daughter to come home. It's almost 10:00 p.m. Where are you, Lisa? You know the rules!
Apr 19 9:58 p.m.

Lisa Henderson I'm at a basketball game. Sorry, Dad. My favorite player is playing. 15 more minutes??
Apr 19 10:02 p.m.

C Read the updates again. Complete the sentences with first names.

1. _____Zack_____ is on vacation.
2. _____ is having dinner.
3. _____ is standing in line.
4. _____ is watching a basketball game.
5. _____ and _____ are students.
6. _____ is studying English.

D Pair work How often do you write messages like the ones above? What do you write about? Tell your partner.

"I love status updates. I write them twice a day. I usually write about the new music I find online."

2 **Writing** My status update

A Write a status update about what you're doing right now or these days.

> *josie9: I'm studying Italian on the weekends.*

B Group work Pass your paper to the classmate on your right. Read and respond to your classmate's update. Continue to pass, read, and respond to each update three times.

> *josie9: I'm studying Italian on the weekends.*
>
> *93arren: I'm not studying Italian, but I'm learning to drive.*

3 **Speaking** Makoto's Desk

Group work Look at Makoto's desk. What do you think he's doing these days?

A: *I think he's studying French.*
B: *Right. And he's taking a painting class.*
C: *Do you think he's drinking a lot of coffee?*

> I can *discuss what people are doing.* ✓

Wrap-up

1 Quick pair review

Lesson A **Do you remember?** Complete the sentences with the correct prepositions. You have one minute.

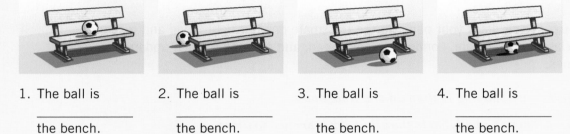

1. The ball is
_____
the bench.

2. The ball is
_____
the bench.

3. The ball is
_____
the bench.

4. The ball is
_____
the bench.

Lesson B **Brainstorm!** Make a list of phone expressions. How many do you know? You have two minutes.

Lesson C **Find out!** What are two things both you and your partner are doing these days? You have one minute.

A: *What are you doing these days?*
B: *I'm taking tango lessons. Are you?*
A: *No, I'm not.*

Lesson D **Guess!** Describe the clothes and actions of someone in your class, but don't say his or her name! Can your partner guess the name? Take turns. You have two minutes.

A: *He's wearing a baseball cap and talking to Angela right now.*
B: *Is it Sebastian?*
A: *Yes, it is.*

2 In the real world

Go to a mall or park. What are people doing? Write about them.

> *People in the Park*
> *I am in the park. Two women are walking. One woman is wearing a red T-shirt. A man is sitting next to me. He is eating his lunch. He is also . . .*

Past experiences

Warm-up

A Look at the pictures. Make three sentences about each one.

B How are *you* different now?

Last weekend

1 **Vocabulary** Weekend activities

A 🔊 Listen and repeat.

listen to music

play basketball

play in a band

shop for new clothes

stay home

stay out late

visit relatives

watch an old movie

B Pair work Do you do any of the activities in Part A? When do you do them?
Tell your partner.

"My friends and I usually play basketball on Saturday mornings."

2 **Language in context** Carmen's weekend

A 🔊 Listen to Carmen talk about last weekend. Number the pictures from 1 to 3.

1. Last Saturday morning, my brother Pedro called me. We talked for hours. I uploaded some photos, and I listened to music.

2. I stayed out late on Saturday night. Pedro and I watched an old movie. We laughed a lot. We loved it!

3. On Sunday afternoon, I stayed home. I watched another movie. I didn't like the ending at all. I cried.

1

B What about you? What do you usually do on weekends?

3 Grammar ◀)) | Simple past regular verbs

I **listened** to music last Saturday.	I **didn't watch** a movie.	*Spelling*
You **stayed** home.	You **didn't stay** out late.	stay → stay**ed**
He **called** me on Saturday.	He **didn't call** me on Sunday.	love → love**d**
We **laughed**.	We **didn't cry**.	cry → cr**ied**
They **stayed** out late.	They **didn't stay** at home.	shop → shop**ped**

A Write sentences about the things Pedro did and didn't do last weekend.

Things to Do

✓ call Carmen   ✗ listen to music

✓ watch a movie   ✓ upload photos

✗ play basketball ✗ shop for new clothes

1. *Pedro called Carmen.*
2. _____
3. _____
4. _____
5. _____
6. _____

B Pair work Make true sentences about your weekend with the past forms of the verbs in Part A. Tell your partner.

4 Pronunciation Simple past -ed endings

A ◀)) Listen and repeat. Notice that some verbs have an extra syllable in the simple past tense.

Same syllable (most verbs)		Extra syllable (verbs ending in *t* and *d*)	
call / called		chat / chat·ted	
listen / listened		start / start·ed	
play / played		upload / upload·ed	

B ◀)) Listen. Complete the chart with the correct verbs.

download / downloaded   shop / shopped   visit / visited

post / posted   stay / stayed   watch / watched

5 Speaking A fun weekend

A Complete the phrases with your own ideas.

chat with _____   exercise _____   study _____   visit _____

cook _____   look for _____   talk to _____   walk to _____

B Pair work Tell your partner about the things you did and didn't do last weekend. Use the phrases from Part A to help you.

A: *I chatted online with my friends last weekend. How about you?*

B: *I didn't chat online with my friends, but I called them.*

6 Keep talking!

Go to page **146** for more practice.

I can *say what I did last weekend.* ☑

You're kidding!

1 Interactions — Expressing surprise

A Look at the pictures. What do you think Ted and Valerie are talking about?

B 🔊 Listen and practice.

Ted: I checked our phone bill this morning.
Valerie: Uh-huh.
Ted: It's usually $59 a month, but this month it's $590.

Valerie: Really? That's not right!
Ted: I know. I didn't pay it. I called the phone company, and they fixed it.
Valerie: Oh, that's good.

C 🔊 Listen to the expressions. Then practice the conversation again with the new expressions.

Showing that you're listening
Uh-huh.
Oh?
Oh, yeah?

Expressing surprise
Really?
What?
You're kidding!

D Check (✓) the best responses. Then practice with a partner.

1. I watched a movie last night.   ✓ Uh-huh.   ☐ Really?
2. I downloaded 500 songs yesterday.   ☐ You're kidding!   ☐ Oh?
3. I didn't study for the big test.   ☐ Oh, yeah?   ☐ What?
4. I played tennis with my friends on Sunday. ☐ You're kidding! ☐ Oh, yeah?

2 Listening What a week!

A 🔊 Listen to Diana tell her friend about the past week. Number the pictures from 1 to 4.

B 🔊 Listen again. What surprises Diana's friend? Complete the sentences.

1. Diana didn't _____**answer**_____ three _____**questions**_____ .
2. Diana's _____ boyfriend _____ her.
3. Julie didn't _____ the _____ .
4. Diana _____ home on _____ .

3 Speaking Really?

A Match the sentences. Then compare with a partner.

1. Last night, I studied for my English test for five hours. __b__
2. I just checked my email. _____
3. Last week, I downloaded two movies. _____
4. On Thursday, I started a new class. _____

a. I watched them with my dad.
b. But I didn't get a good score.
c. I'm learning Chinese.
d. I have 100 new messages.

B **Pair work** Role-play the situations in Part A. Then change roles.

Student A: Say the lines from Part A.
Student B: Show interest or express surprise.

> A: *Last night, I studied for my English test for five hours, but I didn't get a good score.*
> B: *You're kidding! Why not?*

C **Pair work** Role-play new situations. Use your own ideas.

> I can *show that I'm listening.* ☑
> I can *express surprise.* ☑

C *Did you make dinner last night?*

1 **Vocabulary** Things to do

A 🔊 Listen and repeat.

do laundry

do the dishes

get a haircut

go grocery shopping

have a party

make dinner

see a play

see friends

sleep

B **Pair work** How often do you do the things in Part A? Tell your partner.

"I do laundry once a week. I do the dishes every day. . . ."

2 **Conversation** Last night

🔊 Listen and practice.

Mindy: Hi, Pete. Did you see Jennifer last night?
Pete: Yes, I did. But the day didn't go so well.
Mindy: Really? What happened?
Pete: Well, I did my laundry yesterday morning, but my favorite white shirt turned pink.
Mindy: You're kidding!
Pete: Then I got a haircut, but I really didn't like it.
Mindy: Oh, yeah? Did you make dinner for Jennifer?
Pete: Well, I slept for a while, so I didn't go grocery shopping.
Mindy: Oh. Did you eat anything?
Pete: Yeah, we did. Jennifer bought a pizza for us.
Mindy: Really?

3 Grammar 🔊 Simple past irregular verbs; *yes / no* questions

I **saw** Jennifer last night.
She **bought** a pizza.
They **ate** a pizza.

I **didn't see** Jennifer last week.
She **didn't buy** soup.
They **didn't eat** salad.

Did you **see** Jennifer last night?
    Yes, I **did.**   No, I **didn't.**
Did she **buy** dinner?
    Yes, she **did.**   No, she **didn't.**
Did they **eat** dinner?
    Yes, they **did.**   No, they **didn't.**

A Complete the conversation with the simple past tense forms of the verbs. Then practice with a partner.

A: Hey, Pablo. __*Did*__ you __*do*__ (do) today's homework?
B: No, I __*didn't*__ . I _____ (not / have) time.
A: Really? Why not?
B: I _____ (see) some friends yesterday. We _____ (eat) lunch, and then we _____ (go) to the mall.
A: Oh, yeah? _____ you _____ (buy) any clothes?
B: I _____ (not / buy) anything! So, _____ you _____ (do) *your* homework?
A: Yes, I did. And no, you can't see it!

🔊 **Common irregular verbs**

buy → **bought**	have → **had**
do → **did**	make → **made**
drink → **drank**	meet → **met**
drive → **drove**	read → **read**
eat → **ate**	see → **saw**
fall → **fell**	sleep → **slept**
get → **got**	take → **took**
go → **went**	write → **wrote**

Go to page 152 for a list of more irregular verbs.

B Put the words in order to make questions. Then compare with a partner.

1. last night / you / see / did / your friends   *Did you see your friends last night?*
2. go / last weekend / you / did / grocery shopping _____
3. watch / you / a movie / did / last night _____
4. yesterday / stay home / you / did _____
5. make dinner / did / on Thursday / you _____
6. you / did / last Saturday / have a party _____

C Pair work Ask and answer the questions in Part B. Answer with your own information.

A: *Did you see your friends last night?*
B: *Yes, I did. I saw two friends. We ate out at a restaurant.*

4 Speaking Did you?

A Pair work Add two past time expressions to the list. Then ask and answer *Did you . . . ?* questions with each time expression. Take notes.

A: *Did you make dinner last night?*
B: *Yes, I did. Did you do laundry last night?*
A: *No, I didn't.*

Past time expressions	
last night	last week
yesterday	last weekend

B Group work Tell your group about your partner's answers. Did anyone do anything interesting?

5 Keep talking!

Go to page 147 for more practice.

I can talk about routine events in the past.

D | *I saw a great movie.*

1 Reading 🔊

A Do you ever read blogs? What kinds of blogs do you read?

B Read Matt's blog. Who liked the movie?

MATT'S MOVIE REVIEWS

Home | Reviews | Contact Me

Too Young to Love

On Friday, my friend Naomi and I hung out together. We had a very good time. We saw a great old movie at the Cineplex. They are showing old movies all month. Did anyone see "Too Young to Love"? I loved it! It's a story about two young people who are in love. Their parents think they are too young, so they can't get married. It's not a sad movie. It's really funny! We laughed a lot.   Monday, 11:00 a.m.

cgirl: I saw "Too Young to Love." I also saw the play. Both are good. See the movie and the play!
                                                                      Monday, 11:26 a.m.

Oscar: "Too Young to Love"?! You're kidding! I hated the movie, but I liked the music. The sound track had some really good old songs.
                                                                      Monday, 1:00 p.m.

Tomas: My friend and I saw it. She laughed. I cried because I paid for the tickets, and I didn't like it at all.
                                                                      Tuesday, 7:00 a.m.

Joe C: I liked "Too Young to Love." I saw three old movies at the Cineplex last month, and I really liked all of them.
                                                                      Tuesday, 12:45 p.m.

Maria: What?! "Too Young to Love"?! I hated the movie, but I loved the book.
                                                                      Tuesday, 1:15 p.m.

C Read the blog again. Correct the false sentences.

1. Matt saw the movie on ~~Saturday~~. *Matt saw the movie on Friday.*
2. Oscar hated the music. _____
3. Tomas liked *Too Young to Love*. _____
4. Joe C didn't see any movies at the Cineplex last month. _____
5. Maria hated the book *Too Young to Love*. _____

D **Pair work** Do you or your friends ever post your everyday activities on a blog? What do you post? Tell your partner.

"My friend Rosa has a blog. She posts news about her neighborhood once a week."

2 **Writing** A blog post

A Choose one day last week. Complete the chart with information about the things you did that day.

Day	Activities	Places	Other information

B Write a blog post about that day. Use the model and your answers in Part A to help you.

C **Pair work** Share your post. Ask and answer questions for more information.

"Did you have a good time? Did you eat out?"

> *Friday*
> *After class, I met my friend Terry. We went shopping at the mall. I bought a new watch. I didn't pay much for it, but I really like it. I went home at 8:00 p.m.*

3 **Listening** A busy week

A 🔊 Listen to Matt talk about last week. What activities did he do? Check (✓) the correct answers.

- ☐ did laundry
- ✓ got up early
- ☐ got up late
- ☐ made dinner
- ☐ played soccer
- ☐ played the guitar
- ☐ read books
- ☐ stayed out late
- ☐ worked

B 🔊 Listen again. What activities did Matt enjoy? Circle the activities above.

4 **Speaking** I played in a band last year.

A **Class activity** Add two past activities to the chart. Then find classmates who did each thing. Write their names, and ask questions for more information.

Find someone who . . .	Name	Extra information
bought a cell phone last year		
got a haircut last week		
saw a friend yesterday		
made dinner last night		
watched a game on TV last weekend		
wrote a blog post yesterday		

A: *Did you buy a cell phone last year, Alex?*
B: *Yes, I did.*

B Share your information.

"Alex bought a cell phone last year."

> *I can talk about past activities.* ☑

Wrap-up

1 Quick pair review

Lesson A **Find out!** What are three things both you and your partner did after class yesterday? What are three things you didn't do? You have two minutes.

A: *I walked home after class yesterday. Did you?*
B: *Yes, I did. I watched TV at home. Did you?*
A: *No, I didn't. I listened to music.*

Lesson B **Do you remember?** Circle the correct answers. You have two minutes.

1. **A:** I listened to all of Taylor Swift's songs today.
   B: Oh? / (You're kidding!) All of them? She has a lot!

2. **A:** Janet uploaded photos from the party.
   B: Uh-huh. / Really? I know. I looked at them this morning.

3. **A:** Charlie's band played at The Red Room downtown on Saturday night!
   B: What? / Oh? No way! That's so cool! I didn't know that.

4. **A:** I visited my grandmother last weekend.
   B: You're kidding! / Oh, yeah? How is she doing?

Lesson C **Test your partner!** Say eight irregular verbs in the simple present. Can your partner write the simple past forms of the verbs correctly? Check his or her answers. You have two minutes.

1. _____   3. _____   5. _____   7. _____
2. _____   4. _____   6. _____   8. _____

Lesson D **Guess!** Make two true sentences and one false sentence about your activities last week. Can your partner guess the false sentence? Take turns. You have two minutes.

A: *I watched 20 movies last week. I played basketball in the park. I saw a play.*
B: *You didn't watch 20 movies.*
A: *You're right. I only watched 12.*

2 In the real world

Did anyone else do the same things as you yesterday? Go online and find three English-speaking bloggers who did the same activities as you yesterday. Then write about them.

- What activities did both you and the bloggers do yesterday?
- What are the bloggers' names?
- Where are they from?

> *Bloggers and Me*
> *I played basketball yesterday. Three bloggers also played basketball yesterday.*
> *Diego is from California. He played basketball with his brother.*

Getting away

LESSON **A**	LESSON **B**	LESSON **C**	LESSON **D**
• Adjectives • Past of *be*	• Reacting to good news • Reacting to bad news	• Vacation activities • Simple past *Wh-* questions	• Reading: "Travel Tales" • Writing: A postcard

Warm-up

A Do you know any of these places? Which ones?

B What are some popular places to visit in your country? in your city?

Where were you?

1 Vocabulary Adjectives

A 🔊 Listen and repeat.

exciting / fun / great

all right / OK / so-so

awful / terrible

boring

interesting

noisy

quiet

B **Pair work** Think of things that each adjective describes. Discuss your ideas.

A: *Sports are exciting.*
B: *Basketball is exciting, but I think soccer is boring.*

2 Language in context Quick getaways

A 🔊 Listen to four people talk about recent trips. Number the pictures from 1 to 4.

1. We went on a school trip last week. We went to a theater and saw an exciting play. The actors were great.

    – Olivia

2. We just had a three-day weekend. I went away with my family. It was a fun trip, but our hotel wasn't very nice. In fact, it was terrible.

    – Ichiro

3. I was at my brother's apartment last weekend. He doesn't have a TV or a computer. It was quiet and kind of boring.

    – Brian

4. My friend and I went on a day trip last week. We took a local bus to an old town. The bus was awful and noisy, but the trip was interesting. Look what I bought!

    – Eleanor

1

B Did each person like his or her trip? Why or why not?

3 Grammar 🔊 [Past of *be*]

Where were you last weekend?	**Was** your trip interesting?	
I **was** at my brother's apartment.	Yes, it **was**.	No, it **wasn't**.
How was your weekend?	**Were** the people nice?	
It **was** quiet and kind of boring.	Yes, they **were**.	No, they **weren't**.

I / he / she / it	*you / we / they*	*Contractions*	
was	**were**	wasn't = was not	weren't = were not

A Complete the guest comment card with *was, were, wasn't,* or *weren't*. Then compare with a partner.

∽ Guest comments ∾

My wife, son, and I _____ *were* _____ guests at your hotel last week. Unfortunately,
we _____ happy with our room. The room _____ clean, and the
beds _____ awful. And the room _____ near the street. The noise
_____ terrible in the early morning. But the people at the hotel _____
great, so that _____ good!

B Read the answers. Write the questions. Then practice with a partner.

1. *How was your weekend?*   It was great.
2. _____ Yes, my weekend was interesting.
3. _____ I was on a trip.
4. _____ No, I wasn't at the theater on Friday.
5. _____ Yes, I was at home on Sunday afternoon.
6. _____ My parents were in Tahiti.

C Pair work Ask and answer the questions in Part B. Answer with your
own information.

4 Speaking Where were you last Friday night?

A Pair work Interview your partner. Take notes.

Where were you . . . ?	Location	Extra information
at this time yesterday		
on your birthday		
on New Year's Eve		
last Friday night		

B Group work Tell your group about your partner's answers. Who was in an
interesting place? Who did interesting things?

5 Keep talking!

Go to page 148 for more practice.

I can describe where I was in the past. ☑

B | *That's great!*

1 Good news, bad news

A 🔊 Listen and repeat.

I got a promotion.

I lost my wallet.

I missed my flight.

I was sick.

I won a contest.

B Pair work Which things are good news? Which are bad news? Can you think of other examples? Discuss your ideas.

2 Interactions | Reacting to news

A 🔊 Listen and practice.

Meg: Did you have a good weekend?
Joe: Yes! I won a trip in a contest, so I went away last weekend.
Meg: Really? That's great!

Joe: And how was your weekend?
Meg: It wasn't so good. I lost my wallet.
Joe: Oh, no! What happened?

B 🔊 Listen to the expressions. Then practice the conversation again with the new expressions.

Reacting to good news

That's great!
That's excellent!
That's awesome!

Reacting to bad news

Oh, no!
That's too bad.
That's terrible!

C Pair work Practice the conversation again with the examples from Exercise 1. React to the news.

A: *Did you have a good weekend?*
B: *Yes! I got a promotion, so I went shopping.*

3 **Listening** A short trip

A 🔊 Listen to Sam tell a friend about a short trip. Number the pictures from 1 to 6.

B 🔊 Listen again. Was Sam's trip great, good, bad, or awful?

4 **Speaking** That's . . . !

A Write three good things and three bad things that happened to you last week.

	Good things that happened	Bad things that happened
1.		
2.		
3.		

B **Class activity** Ask your classmates about their week. React to the news.

A: *Did you do anything interesting last week?*
B: *Well, I started a new job.*
A: *That's excellent!*
B: *Yeah. But I lost my cell phone.*
A: *That's terrible!*

I can **react to news.** ☑

C   *My vacation*

1 **Vocabulary** Vacation activities

A 🔊 Listen and repeat.

buy souvenirs   go sightseeing   go to a festival   go to the beach

relax   shop in markets   take a tour   take pictures

B Pair work Did you do any of the activities in Part A on your last vacation? Tell your partner.

"On my last vacation, I bought souvenirs and took pictures. I didn't go to the beach."

2 **Conversation** Back from vacation

🔊 Listen and practice.

Dave: How was your vacation, Kate?
Kate: Oh, it was exciting. We had a great time.
Dave: Where did you go?
Kate: I went to Veracruz, Mexico.
Dave: That's great. Who did you travel with?
Kate: My sister.
Dave: When did you get back?
Kate: Last night. I got home at midnight.
Dave: Really? That's late! So, what did you do there?
Kate: Well, we went to a festival called *Carnaval*. We also shopped in local markets and took lots of pictures. Look, I bought you a souvenir.
Dave: Thanks! I love it!

3 Grammar 🔊 | Simple past *Wh-* questions

Where did you **go** on vacation?
   I went to Veracruz, Mexico.
When did you **get** back?
   Last night.
Who did you **travel** with?
   My sister.

What did you **do** there?
   We went to a festival and shopped.
Why did you **go** to Veracruz?
   Because the festival is famous.
How did you **get** to Veracruz?
   By plane.

Match the questions and the answers. Then practice with a partner.

1. Where did you go on vacation? __*f*__
2. Who did you go with? _____
3. When did you get back? _____
4. What did you do on vacation? _____
5. Why did you go to Vietnam? _____
6. How did you travel in Vietnam? _____

a. We got back last week.
b. We took the bus and the train.
c. We relaxed and took pictures.
d. Because I have friends there.
e. I went with my brother.
f. I went to Vietnam.

4 Pronunciation Reduction of *did you*

A 🔊 Listen and repeat. Notice how *did you* is pronounced /dɪdʒə/ after *Wh-* question words.

Where **did you** go?   What **did you** do?   When **did you** get back?

B Pair work Practice the questions in the grammar chart. Reduce *did you* to /dɪdʒə/ after *Wh-* question words.

5 Speaking What a vacation!

A Answer the questions.

- Where did you go on your last vacation? _____
- Who did you go with? _____
- When did you go? _____
- What did you do there? _____
- How did you travel? _____
- Did you buy anything? _____
- What did you like about the vacation? _____
- What didn't you like about the vacation? _____

B Group work Tell your group about your last vacation. Ask and answer questions for more information.

fly → flew

6 Keep talking!

Go to page 149 for more practice.

take a boat → took a boat

I can *talk about my last vacation.* ☑

111

D *Travel experiences*

1 Reading 🔊

A How often do you go on vacation? Where do you go?

B Read the travel blog posts. What country is each person visiting?

travel tales

I'm here in Chiang Mai, Thailand. Yesterday, I went on a short elephant ride. There was a man on the elephant in front of me. His name was Alan Johnson. My name is Alan Johnson, too! _____

Alan Johnson   Posted on October 12, 10:30 a.m.

My sister and I are in Paris, France. It's our first trip overseas. We went to an outdoor café the other day, and Johnny Depp was at the next table. How exciting! _____

Mary O'Connor   Posted on October 14, 6:48 p.m.

I'm here with my parents at a hotel in Miami, Florida. We came to visit our relatives. We all went to bed last night at about midnight. At 3:00 in the morning, we heard a fire alarm. _____

Anita Gonzalez   Posted on October 15, 8:06 a.m.

I'm in Granada, Nicaragua. I came here to help build houses. It's a great country. We finished our first house yesterday. We're not staying in a hotel. We're staying in a school. ___*1*___

Diane Nicholson   Posted on October 21, 9:12 p.m.

C Read the blog posts again. What is the last sentence of each post? Number the posts from 1 to 4.

1. Last night, we all slept in one big room!

2. He was nice to us, and I have a cool photo now.

3. I can't believe that we have the same name!

4. We ran down to the street and were fine.

D **Pair work** What adjectives describe each travel experience? Discuss your ideas.

A: *I think Alan Johnson's trip was very exciting!*
B: *Me, too. I love elephants, and Thailand is an interesting country.*

2 **Listening** Three different trips

A 🔊 Listen to three people talk about their vacations. How do they describe them?
Check (✓) the correct answers.

	How were their vacations?		What was one thing they liked?
1.	☐ awful	✓ great	*shopping*
	☐ boring	☐ so-so	
2.	☐ fun	☐ OK	
	☐ interesting	☐ terrible	
3.	☐ awful	☐ exciting	
	☐ boring	☐ great	

B 🔊 Listen again. What did they like about their trips? Write one thing for each
person in the chart.

3 **Writing and speaking** A postcard

A Read Sofia's postcard to Jack about her vacation.

Dear Jack,

Linda and I are having a great time
here in Morocco. We took a train from
Casablanca to Marrakech yesterday.
Last night, we went to a big "souk," or
market. We walked around the market for
hours! I bought a nice souvenir for you!

See you soon!
Sofia

B Write a postcard to a friend or family member about an experience
you had on vacation. Use the model in Part A to help you.

C Class activity Post your postcards around the room. Read your classmates'
postcards. Then write questions about five postcards that interest you.

1. Eddie – What did you buy for your sister?

2. Jung-woo – Who did you travel with?

3. Marcus – When did you take this vacation?

D Class activity Find the classmates who wrote the five postcards.
Ask them your questions.

A: *Eddie, what did you buy your sister?*
B: *I bought a scarf.*
A: *I see, thanks. Excuse me, Jung-woo, who did you travel with?*

I can *describe a vacation.* ☑

Wrap-up

1 Quick pair review

Lesson A **Brainstorm!** Make a list of adjectives. How many do you know? You have one minute.

Lesson B **Do you remember?** Check (✓) the correct answers. You have one minute.

1. I won a free ticket to Jamaica. ☑ That's great! ☐ Oh, no!
2. I lost my cell phone. ☐ That's terrible! ☐ That's excellent!
3. My sister missed her flight. ☐ That's awesome. ☐ That's too bad.
4. Charlie met Leonardo DiCaprio. ☐ Oh, no! ☐ That's great!

Lesson C **Find out!** What are two things both you and your partner did on your last vacation? You have two minutes.

A: *Did you go sightseeing on your last vacation?*
B: *Yes, I did. How about you?*
A: *Yes, I went sightseeing, too.*

Lesson D **Test your partner!** Describe a vacation. Can your partner draw a postcard of your vacation? Check his or her drawing. You have two minutes.

"Last year, my sister and I went to Madrid, Spain. We shopped in El Rastro Market and went to art museums."

2 In the real world

Do you ever read travel blogs? Go online and find a travel blog in English. Then write about it.

- Where did the blogger go?
- When did he or she go there?
- What did he or she do there?

> *Kelly's Travel Blog*
> *Kelly is a blogger from Canada. Last week, she went on vacation to Scotland. She went sightseeing in Glasgow. She went to . . .*

Time to celebrate

Warm-up

graduation

A Label the pictures with the correct words.

> birthday ✓graduation holiday wedding

B What special events do you celebrate?

1 **Vocabulary** Months and dates

A ◀))) Listen and repeat.

January	February	March	April	May	June
July	August	September	October	November	December

1st first	**9th** ninth	**17th** seventeenth	**25th** twenty-fifth
2nd second	**10th** tenth	**18th** eighteenth	**26th** twenty-sixth
3rd third	**11th** eleventh	**19th** nineteenth	**27th** twenty-seventh
4th fourth	**12th** twelfth	**20th** twentieth	**28th** twenty-eighth
5th fifth	**13th** thirteenth	**21st** twenty-first	**29th** twenty-ninth
6th sixth	**14th** fourteenth	**22nd** twenty-second	**30th** thirtieth
7th seventh	**15th** fifteenth	**23rd** twenty-third	**31st** thirty-first
8th eighth	**16th** sixteenth	**24th** twenty-fourth	

B Class activity When is your birthday? Stand in the order of your birthdays, from the first to the last in the year.

A: *My birthday is July twenty-eighth.*
B: *Mine is July twentieth. You're next to me.*

2 **Language in context** Special days

A ◀))) Listen to three people talk about special days. What are the dates of the special days?

I'm going to graduate from high school on June 8th. I'm going to start college in September.

– *Sarah*

My eightieth birthday is on August 21st. I'm going to go skydiving for the first time. I can't wait!

– *Walter*

My boyfriend, Kenta, and I are going to get married on October 16th. We're going to have a big wedding.

– *Mari*

B What about you? What days of the year are special to you? Why?

3 Grammar ◀))) **Be going to; yes / no questions**

I'm **going to graduate** on June 8th. I'm **not going to start** college in July.	**Are** you **going to start** college? Yes, I am. No, I'm not.
Walter**'s going to go** skydiving. He**'s not going to play** basketball.	**Is** Walter **going to go** skydiving? Yes, he is. No, he isn't.
Mari and Kenta **are going to get** married. They**'re not going to have** a small wedding.	**Are** they **going to have** a big wedding? Yes, they are. No, they aren't.

A Complete the conversation with the correct forms of *be going to*.
Then practice with a partner.

A: __Are__ you _going to graduate_ (graduate) from college
this year?

B: Yeah, on May 30th. My parents _____
(have) a big party for me.

A: Great! _____ the party _____ (be) at
their house?

B: No, it _____ (not / be) at the house.
They _____ (have) it at a restaurant.

A: _____ you _____ (get) a job right away?

B: No, I'm not. First, I _____ (travel).
Then I _____ (look) for a job.

B Pair work Ask and answer three *Are you going to . . . ?* questions.
Answer with your own information.

4 Pronunciation Reduction of *going to* before verbs

A ◀))) Listen and repeat. Notice how *going to* is reduced to /gənə/ in informal
spoken English.

Are you **going to** do anything special?   Yes. I'm **going to** go skydiving.

B Pair work Practice the sentences in the grammar chart. Reduce *going to*
to /gənə/.

5 Speaking Three special days

A Write the dates and your plans for three special days or holidays next year.

	Special day: _____	Special day: _____	Special day: _____
Dates			
Plans			

B Pair work Tell your partner about your special days. Ask and answer questions
for more information.

6 Keep talking!

Go to page 150 for more practice.

I can talk about my plans for specific dates. ☑

B *Sure. I'd love to.*

1 Interactions Invitations

A How often do you go to the movies with your friends?

B 🔊 Listen and practice.

Bill: Hello?
Brandon: Hey, Bill. It's Brandon. Listen, do you want to see a movie tonight?
Bill: Tonight? I'm sorry. I can't.
Brandon: Oh, OK. Well, maybe some other time.

Melissa: Hello?
Brandon: Hi, Melissa. This is Brandon. Do you want to see a movie tonight?
Melissa: A movie? Sure. I'd love to.
Brandon: Great.

C 🔊 Listen to the expressions. Then practice the conversation again with the new expressions.

Declining an invitation
I'm sorry. I can't.
I'm afraid I can't.
I'm really sorry, but I can't.

Accepting an invitation
Sure. I'd love to.
Sounds good.
Yeah. That sounds great.

D Pair work Practice the conversations again with the activities below.

get some ice cream   hang out   play video games   watch a DVD

A: *Hello?*
B: *Hey, Bill. It's Brandon. Listen, do you want to get some ice cream tonight?*

2 Listening I'd love to, but . . .

A 🔊 Listen to four people invite their friends to do things tonight. Number the pictures from 1 to 4.

B 🔊 Listen again. Do the friends accept or decline the invitations? Check (✓) the correct answers.

1. ☑ accept   2. ☐ accept   3. ☐ accept   4. ☐ accept
   ☐ decline   ☐ decline   ☐ decline   ☐ decline

3 Speaking Do you want to hang out?

Class activity "Call" your classmates and invite them to do something with you right now. Your classmates accept the invitations or decline them with excuses. Use the ideas below or your own ideas.

Possible things to do	Possible excuses	Responses to excuses
go out for coffee	I'm cooking dinner.	Oh, that's OK.
go to a party	I'm not feeling well.	Maybe next time.
see a movie	I'm eating lunch.	I'm sorry you can't make it.
go to the mall	I'm studying for an exam.	OK, I understand.
hang out	I'm doing my homework.	That's all right.
go shopping	I'm working late tonight.	No problem.

A: *Hello?*
B: *Hi, it's me. Do you want to go to the mall?*
A: *I'm really sorry, but I can't. I'm not feeling well.*
B: *OK, I understand. Maybe next time.*

I can *accept or decline an invitation.* ☑

Planning a party

1 Vocabulary Party checklist

A 🔊 Match the things on the checklist and the pictures. Then listen and check your answers.

THINGS TO DO

1. ☑ *g* *bake a cake*
2. ☐ *buy a gift*
3. ☐ *choose the music*
4. ☐ *decorate the room*
5. ☐ *make a guest list*
6. ☐ *plan the menu*
7. ☐ *prepare the food*
8. ☐ *send invitations*

a John
Hee-jin
Miguel

b Invitation

c Menu
Sandwiches
Ice Cream
Soda

d

e HAPPY BIRTHDAY

f

g

h

B **Pair work** When is a good time to do each thing in Part A? Discuss your ideas.

| 2 weeks before the party | 2–3 days before the party | the morning of the party |
| 1 week before the party | the day before the party | 1 hour before the party |

"A good time to make a guest list is two weeks before the party."

2 Conversation I can bake!

🔊 Listen and practice.

Andrea: We have a lot of things to do for Eric's birthday party. Look, I made a checklist.
Mark: Good idea. Who's going to help us?
Andrea: Rosario. She's going to send the invitations.
Mark: How is she going to send them?
Andrea: By email.
Mark: Good. That's easy. What are we going to buy for Eric?
Andrea: Let's get him a sweater.
Mark: Great. Who's going to bake the cake?
Andrea: I'm going to bake it.
Mark: Um, do you think that's a good idea?
Andrea: Hey, I can bake!
Mark: OK.

3 Grammar 🔊 **Wh- questions with *be going to*; object pronouns**

What are we going to buy **Eric**?	Let's get **him** a sweater.
Who's going to bake **the cake**?	Andrea's going to bake **it**.
How is she going to send **the invitations**?	She's going to send **them** by email.

Subject	I	you	he	she	it	we	they
Object	me	you	him	her	it	us	them

A Complete the conversation with the correct forms of *be going to*. Then practice with a partner.

A: What time __*are*__ you __*going to go*__ (go) to Eric's birthday party?
B: I _____ (go) to the party at 6:45.
A: How _____ you _____ (get) there?
B: My friend Jason _____ (drive). Do you want a ride?
A: Um, sure, thanks! What _____ you _____ (do) after the party?
B: Jason and I _____ (go) out. I think we _____ (see) a movie.

B Rewrite the sentences. Use object pronouns. Then compare with a partner.

1. He's not going to invite Mary. __*He's not going to invite her.*_____
2. Let's call Bill and Ami again. _____
3. I'm going to see Eric tomorrow. _____
4. He's going to help Debbie and me. _____
5. We're going to buy the present tomorrow. _____
6. Call Rosario at 5:00. _____

C Class activity Ask your classmates what they're going to do tonight. Answer with your own information.

4 Speaking Let's decide together.

A Pair work Discuss the situations.

| Your classmate Masao is in the hospital. He has nothing to do. What are you going to bring him? | You're planning your friend's birthday party. Where is it going to be? What are you going to eat and drink? | You want music for your teacher's birthday party. What songs are you going to play? How are you going to listen to them? |

A: *What are we going to bring to Masao?*
B: *Let's bring him a new video game.*
A: *That's a great idea. How about . . . ?*

B Group work Share your ideas with another pair. Ask and answer questions for more information.

5 Keep talking!

Go to page 151 for more practice.

I can *discuss and agree on plans.* ✓

D | Birthdays

1 Reading 🔊

A What was the last party you went to? What did you do at the party?

B Read the article. Which birthdays are special in each country?

Birthday Traditions
around the world

Nigeria
In Nigeria, the first, fifth, tenth, and fifteenth birthdays are very special. To celebrate these birthdays, people have big parties and invite up to 100 people. They eat "jollof rice." This is rice with tomatoes, red peppers, onions, and cassava, a kind of potato.

Japan
The third, fifth, and seventh birthdays are very important in Japan. Every year on November 15th, children of these ages celebrate the *Shichi-go-san* (Seven-five-three) Festival. They usually wear traditional clothes and eat "thousand-year candy" for a long life.

Ecuador
In Ecuador, a family has a big party when a girl turns 15 years old. The birthday girl wears a dress, and her father puts her first pair of high-heeled shoes on her. Then he dances with her. Fourteen other girls dance with fourteen other boys at the same time.

South Korea
Parents in South Korea sometimes try to guess a child's future on his or her first birthday. They put the child in front of some objects, such as a book and a coin. They wait to see which object the child takes. For example, a book means the child is going to be a teacher. A coin means the child is going to have a lot of money.

C Read the article again. Answer the questions.

1. On special birthdays, what do Nigerian children eat? <u>*They eat "jollof rice."*</u>
2. Who celebrates *Shichi-go-san*? _____
3. Who dances with a 15-year-old Ecuadorian girl at her birthday party? _____
4. How do South Korean parents guess a child's future? _____

D Pair work How did you celebrate your last birthday? Tell your partner.

"I celebrated my last birthday with my friends. We ate out at a nice restaurant."

122

2 Listening Sweet 16

A 🔊 Listen to Amanda, a 16-year-old American girl, describe her "Sweet 16" birthday party. Check (✓) the true sentences.

1. ✓ Amanda's birthday is July 14th.

2. ☐ ~~Her parents~~ *She* made a guest list.

3. ☐ She sent the invitations.

4. ☐ She and her father decorated the room.

5. ☐ She had pizza, ice cream, and cake.

6. ☐ Forty of her friends came.

7. ☐ She got a gift from her parents.

8. ☐ She's going to have a party on her 18th birthday.

B 🔊 Listen again. Correct the false sentences.

3 Writing A thank-you note

A Think of a birthday gift (or any gift) you received. Answer the questions.

- What is the gift? _____
- Who is it from? _____
- Why did you get it? _____
- What do you like about it? _____

Dear Liz,

Thanks a lot for the birthday gift. I love the sweater. Blue and green are my favorite colors. Thank you for coming to my party!

Thanks again,
Sun-hee

B Write a thank-you note for the gift. Use the model and your answers in Part A to help you.

C Group work Share your thank-you notes. Did any of you write about similar gifts?

4 Speaking How we celebrate

A Group work Discuss the ways people celebrate birthdays in your culture. Use the questions below and your own ideas.

- Which birthdays are very special?
- Do people celebrate with family, friends, or both?
- What do people eat and drink?
- What do people do?
- Do they give gifts? What kinds of gifts?
- How do you usually celebrate birthdays?

B Group work Tell your group how you are going to celebrate your next birthday. Are you going to do any of the things you discussed in Part A?

a birthday party in Mexico

I can describe birthday traditions in my culture. ☑

Wrap-up

1 Quick pair review

Lesson A Guess! Say three dates when you are going to do something special. Can your partner guess what you are going to do? Take turns. You have three minutes.

A: *I'm going to do something special on June 17th.*
B: *Are you going to graduate?*
A: *Yes, I am!*

Lesson B Do you remember? Read the sentences. Write A (accepting an invitation), D (declining an invitation), or E (making an excuse). You have one minute.

1. I'd love to. _____
2. I'm studying for an exam. _____
3. That sounds great. _____
4. I'm really sorry, but I can't. _____
5. I'm working late tonight. _____
6. I'm afraid I can't. _____

Lesson C Brainstorm! Make a list of things you do to plan a party. How many do you know? You have two minutes.

Lesson D Find out! What are three activities both you and your partner do on your birthdays? You have two minutes.

A: *I eat cake on my birthday. Do you?*
B: *Yes, I eat cake, too.*

2 In the real world

When is your birthday? Go online and find information in English about two important events that happened that day. Then write about them.

- Where did the events happen?
- Who participated in the events?
- Why were the events important?

> *My Birthday*
> *My birthday is December 17th. On this day in 1903, the Wright brothers flew an airplane for 12 seconds. This was important because . . .*

What's in your shopping basket?

A Choose seven items to put into your shopping basket. Circle them.

B Pair work Find out what is in your partner's basket. Can you make the dishes below with the food in your baskets?

Stew
beef
carrots
noodles

Fruit smoothie
apples
bananas
milk

Spaghetti and meatballs
beef
cheese
pasta
tomatoes

A: *I have beef and noodles. Do you have any carrots?*
B: *Yes, I do. We can make stew!*

C Pair work What else can you make with the food in your baskets?

How often do you eat standing up?

Group work Add two eating habits to the list. Then discuss how often you do each thing.

drink coffee in the morning

drink tea

eat alone

eat candy in class

eat fast food for breakfast

eat on the street

eat standing up

_____
(your own idea)

_____
(your own idea)

A: *Do you ever drink coffee in the morning?*
B: *Yes, I do.*
C: *How often do you drink coffee in the morning?*
B: *I drink coffee in the morning three times a week. How about you?*

What's missing?

Student A

A **Pair work** You and your partner have pictures of the same neighborhood, but different places are missing. Ask questions to get the names. Write them.

A: *What's across from the post office?*
B: *The gas station.*

B **Pair work** Cover the picture. Tell your partner six things you remember.

A: *The gas station is across from the post office.*
B: *That's right.*

What's missing?

Student B

A **Pair work** You and your partner have pictures of the same neighborhood, but different places are missing. Ask questions to get the names. Write them.

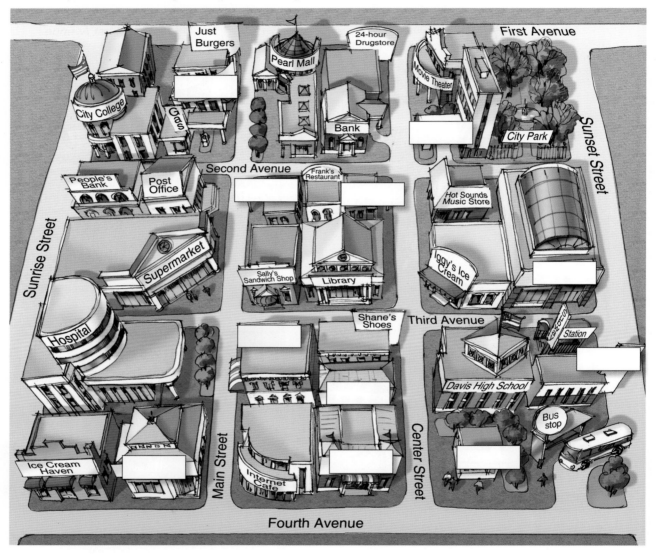

A: *What's next to the movie theater?*
B: *Parkview Hotel.*

B **Pair work** Cover the picture. Tell your partner six things you remember.

A: *Parkview Hotel is next to the movie theater.*
B: *That's right.*

An unusual zoo

Pair work What's wrong at this zoo? Make ten sentences about the people, animals, and other things in the zoo. Use *There is . . .* , *There are . . .* , and prepositions of location.

"There's a bear in the car."

Neighbors

A **Pair work** Look through the windows. What are the people doing? Discuss your ideas.

A: *I think the man is doing his homework. What do you think?*
B: *I think he's writing a letter. He's sitting, too.*

B **Pair work** What are the people actually doing? Go to page 153 to check your answers.

Who is it?

A Write three sentences about what you're doing these days on three pieces of paper. Don't write your name!

I'm tutoring a student.	*I'm taking tennis lessons.*	*I'm not studying every night!*

B **Group work** Put your papers on the table. Take one paper and read the sentences. Your group guesses the name. Take turns.

A: *This person is tutoring a student.*
B: *Is it Juliana?*
C: *No, it's not me!*
D: *Is it Kate?*

C **Group work** Discuss the activities you're doing these days. Ask and answer questions for more information.

A: *Who are you tutoring these days, Ken?*
B: *I'm tutoring a friend of mine. His name is Luke.*
C: *Are you tutoring him in English?*
B: *No, I'm not. I'm tutoring him in Japanese.*

Picture story

A Pair work Look at the pictures of John and Alice Gordon. What did they do last weekend? Use the verbs to discuss your ideas.

clean	fix	play	stay out	watch
dance	paint	shop for	study	

A: *John and Alice cleaned the house.*
B: *Alice fixed her bike.*

B Pair work Cover the pictures. What did John and Alice do last weekend? Answer with the information you remember.

Memories

Group work Make five true sentences about your past activities with the phrases below. Your group asks three questions about each sentence for more information. Take turns.

Yesterday	Last night	Last weekend	Last month	Last year
I drank . . .	I ate . . .	I saw . . .	I bought . . .	I went . . .
I got up . . .	I went to bed . . .	I had . . .	I read . . .	I met . . .
I did . . .	I slept . . .	I drove . . .	I made . . .	I took . . .

A: *Last night, I ate soup for dinner.*
B: *Did you eat in a restaurant?*
A: *No, I didn't. I ate at home.*
C: *Did you make the soup?*
A: *No, I didn't. My son made it.*
D: *Did you . . . ?*

School trips

A **Pair work** Add three more questions about school or work trips to the list. Then interview your partner. Take notes.

1. What was your favorite school or work trip?
   _____

2. How old were you?
   _____

3. How was the trip?
   _____

4. Was there anything bad about the trip?
   _____

5. Did you take a bus there?
   _____

6. Were you there all day?
   _____

7. Did you buy anything?
   _____

8. _____
   _____

9. _____
   _____

10. _____
    _____

B **Pair work** Tell another classmate about your partner's answers.

*"Michi's favorite school trip was to a cookie factory. She was ten years old.
The trip was . . ."*

What a vacation!

A Look at the items from Maggie's vacation. Write five questions and answers about her vacation.

1. *Where did Maggie go on vacation?*
   New York City.
2. *What kind of music did she hear?*
   Jazz music.

B Group work Cover the picture. Ask your questions. How many correct answers did your group get?

This weekend

A Make eight true sentences about your plans with the phrases below.

My plans		
	dress up	
	eat out	
	go to a concert	tonight
	go to bed late	this evening
I'm going to	go to the mall	tomorrow
I'm not going to	go window-shopping	this weekend
	hang out	next Monday
	study	next Friday
	watch a movie	
	work	

dress up

go to a concert

go window-shopping

B **Pair work** Tell your partner about your plans. Ask and answer questions for more information.

A: *I'm going to go to bed late tonight.*
B: *Are you going to watch a movie tonight?*
A: *No, I'm not. I'm going to study.*

Party planners

A **Group work** Plan an end-of-class party. Take notes.

Date of party	Time of party	Place of party

Food and drink	Decorations	Music

A: *When are we going to have our party?*
B: *Let's have it after class on Friday at 8:00.*
C: *OK. Now, where are we going to have it?*
D: *Let's have it here at the school.*

B **Class activity** Share your ideas. Ask and answer questions for more information.

A: *We're going to have our party on Friday at 8:00.*
B: *It's going to be here at our school.*
C: *Which room is the party going to be in?*

C **Class activity** Vote for your favorite plan.

Irregular verbs

Base form	Simple past
be	was, were
become	became
build	built
buy	bought
can	could
choose	chose
come	came
do	did
draw	drew
drink	drank
drive	drove
eat	ate
fall	fell
feel	felt
fly	flew
get	got
give	gave
go	went
hang	hung
have	had
hear	heard
hold	held
know	knew
leave	left

Base form	Simple past
lose	lost
make	made
meet	met
pay	paid
read	read
ride	rode
run	ran
say	said
see	saw
sell	sold
send	sent
sing	sang
sit	sat
sleep	slept
speak	spoke
spend	spent
stand	stood
swim	swam
take	took
teach	taught
think	thought
wear	wore
win	won
write	wrote

Answer key

Keep talking! Neighbors

Credits

CAMBRIDGE UNIVERSITY PRESS
Cambridge, New York, Melbourne, Madrid, Cape Town,
Singapore, São Paulo, Delhi, Mexico City

Cambridge University Press
32 Avenue of the Americas, New York, NY 10013-2473, USA

www.cambridge.org
Information on this title: www.cambridge.org/9780521126601

© Cambridge University Press 2011

First published 2011
2nd printing 2013

Printed in Hong Kong, China, by Golden Cup Printing Company Limited

A catalog record for this publication is available from the British Library.

ISBN 978-0-521-12657-1 Student's Book 1A with Self-study CD-ROM
ISBN 978-0-521-12660-1 Student's Book 1B with Self-study CD-ROM
ISBN 978-0-521-12649-6 Workbook 1A
ISBN 978-0-521-12652-6 Workbook 1B
ISBN 978-0-521-12646-5 Teacher's Edition 1 with Assessment Audio CD / CD-ROM
ISBN 978-0-521-12640-3 Class Audio CDs 1
ISBN 978-0-521-12619-9 Classware 1
ISBN 978-0-521-12638-0 DVD 1

For a full list of components, visit www.cambridge.org/fourcorners

Art direction, book design, photo research, and layout services: Adventure House, NYC
Audio production: CityVox, NYC
Video production: Steadman Productions

Four Corners

Jack C. Richards · David Bohlke

1B

Student's Book

520 869 78 7